THE HEART'S PANGAEA

Wick Poetry Chapbook Series
Maggie Anderson, Editor

THE HEART'S PANGAEA

Susan Neale

The Kent State University Press

Kent, Ohio, & London, England

Library of Congress Catalog Card Number 95-20500
ISBN 0-87338-545-4
Manufactured in the United States of America

05 04 03 02 01 00 99 98 97   6 5 4 3 2

The Wick Poetry Chapbook series is sponsored by the Stan and Tom Wick
Poetry Program and the Department of English at Kent State University.

Library of Congress Cataloging-in-Publication Data
Neale, Susan, 1963–
    The heart's pangaea / Susan Neale.   ∞
       p.   cm. — (Wick poetry chapbook series ; no. 10)
    ISBN 0-87338-545-4 (pbk. : alk. paper)
    I. Title.   II. Series.
PS3564.E218H4   1996
811'.54—dc20   95-20500

British Library Cataloging-in-Publication data are available.

Pangaea, the supercontinent of Wegener's Continental Drift Theory, was a single landmass until the Cretaceous (136–65 M.Y.). The landmass aggregated about 240 million years ago and remained intact for 100 million years. It was surrounded by the Panthalassa Ocean which covered the rest of the Earth.

When Pangaea broke up, volcanoes arose in the rifts which widened a few centimeters a year. The landmass was split by the Tethys Sea into Laurasia and Gondwana. These great continents later split into 6 blocks, the present continents.

CONTENTS

ACKNOWLEDGMENTS

Grateful acknowledgment is made to the *Ohio State Alumni Magazine,* in which the following poems first appeared: "Bereft," "Miscarriage," "Lament for Pangaea," and "Fellow Traveler."

I would like to thank Maggie Anderson for her fine and patient editing. Many thanks also to all those who inspired these poems.

BEREFT

Everywhere we have been since beginning
Is mapped in the memory somewhere.
My mind holds scores of useless diagrams:
Where the bleach is in the grocery store in Tucson,
Where to park on Sundays in the District, or how
Each apartment of our marriage had a hiding place
And a certain spot of sunlight, good for reading;
How the sunlight moved across smooth boards and
    splinters,
Park and Lombardy, third flight, ninth stair:
Your homecoming creak. Flowers, left behind,
Each planting sketched in pencil,
Became other people's gardens, year after year.
The stoves: which burners worked. The dishes
That moved with us, broke,
Were replaced, and broke again.
I still have one fork from the first pattern,
And a handful of seeds from the last garden.
At night, I dream I am riding
The bicycle paths of my childhood;
I awake to your absent outline.
Yes, I remember, deep in some part,
As Africa yearns for Brazil,
I could chart the arch of your feet,
The smooth places, tenor of tendons,
The three colors needed to paint you:
Alizarin, umber, burnt sienna;
The rhythm of heart against breath,
The pattern of movement in sleep,
The shape of your jaw, the story to every scar;

The hold of your hands on my body,
And where you were likely to touch first,
With what weight, with what words.
How long will these things ride the surface
Before sinking into the dark silt?
Each day, the shoreline is farther.
Now my own shape seems a riddle, peculiar.
I watch the picture fade:
The day we struck out for the desert,
You with the keys, me with the map in my hands.

MISCARRIAGE

She gave him a plant and he killed it.
Didn't mean to, of course. Hoped she wouldn't
Find the dead, burnt-dry bowl, leaves withered
Into black curls. It had been a wedding gift,
And he promiséd to take care of it, but
The desert confounded him.

They are hiking together now,
In the mountains, in New Mexico. Hiking
Past prickly pear, toward the gray cliffs,
Under swaying arms of ocotillo.
A pink blister puffs out her heel.
They bathe in a cool stream:
Naked, with glasses on,
He fishes out an oval stone.

That night they search out a secret path,
Find it in the dark. The morning sends
Sunlight peeling up their green hill,
Striking aspens and papery wild iris.
Thistledown lights in the air.

They stand together on the cliff,
Looking down at the desert.
In her pocket are sunflower seeds, and
The small, cold hammer to crack the geode.
She'll give him half:
A cup of diamonds, new to this world.

KALENDARIUM

I am forever crescent, told my thin shell
Makes waves rise, breaks rainstorms,
Drives bees to hive, ripens tomatoes at night.
In fact, I do none of these things:
Never wax full, stun morning glories open;
Never cast shadows to make two of you,
Startling pale colors from the sleeping earth,
Bringing women strange pains for no reason.
Nothing can germinate in this thin light.
Busheled by the cold, empty side I rise,
And no wolf howls, no mockingbird will sing.
Slick sickle: I've put a rein on the winds.

HEALING THE HOUSE

Last night I went back to our one-bedroom house in
   Tucson
And made things happen I'd wanted to happen.

I swept clean the red cement floor in the moonlight.
I washed the walls and painted them white.

A carpet of ochre and cinnamon,
A painting of rows of green corn—

He didn't like things on the wall, but this wasn't for him.
For curtains, I painted gold stars on white scrim,

Forged a curtain rod of iron, curved in viney tendrils,
And held the fabric back with iron spirals.

I laughed at how much I could do by myself,
As boxes of new books spilled into new shelves.

Ivy and blue glass bottles graced the window
Above an oak bed from Mexico,

The headboard, golden-grained, carved in flowers;
White eyelet sheets, white pillows, white comforter.

The sun sifted in, dappled the bed with stars;
Across it, a book, a cat that never was ours.

Let me remember this, instead of the cold
That seeped through the floor. And the hardness
   of the floor.

PORTULACAS

Maybe you forgot you planted them.
You stub your vision on their sudden colors,
Colors of houses in dreams, houses
In Mediterranean towns,
Their bright blue doors spilling open
To backyards on cliff edges,
Or sprawling to steep alleys
Giving way to icy gray mountains.
You turn a corner into the market
Where someone is calling your name:
"Come here," she says. "Come here,
I have something to give you."
The old woman is your mother's mother's mother.
"This must be the motherland," you say.
She laughs and wraps you in a shining orange shawl,
And the processional dancers sweep down from the hills
Like sudden rain, carrying you in their tide of song
To the sea, where each child will press
A starfish in your palm: aqua, magenta, yellow.
All the men and the women of the village
Are lining the rim of the canyon:
"Come and stay with us," they call.
"Never stop looking for me," you answer.

AFTER READING NERUDA

The sun pulls gently away from us,
changing the colors, casting everything golden.
I can read no more in this light.
Outside, on the patio, Spanish guitar;
a song about bodies, skin and pleasure,
and orange trees hanging heavy,
at night on *los bancos del río*.

I want to go back to the place
where flowers bloomed vanilla
into the air, and the touch of your arm
on my shoulder did not make me cry.
Your dark brown eyes were like the river:
we swam under the moon,
our bodies rippling the water.
When I say *bodies* I mean your arms,
climbing the ladder of sky,
twining with my arms, curved
anthers of lilies. I mean
the edges gone, touching
and gone.

Now I am holding on to the last of Neruda,
the rhythms lilting like the guitar's *paseo*.
If only our language had so many o's for its endings.
Instead, what we say to each other
clanks and thumps like forks in a drawer,
dull sounds that don't fit love, or mourning.
Everything we say rings mundane or profane:
When I say *body* you picture a dead one,
when what I want you to see is a lover,
shoulders touched by sunlight,
naked on the bank of the river.

El corazón sings in the quiet times,
when I am in the bath, before falling asleep,
or, on a Sunday, when I wake up in sunlight
with nowhere to go immediately. I hear her beat:
Oh corazón perdido
en mí mismo, en mi propia investidura,
qué generosa transición te puebla!

DREAM REMEMBERED OVER
A CUP OF RED ROSE TEA

Delicious to remember even the dream of it:
I'm singing because they asked me to,
on the wrap-around stairway landing,
like an opera star on her balcony, and everywhere
friends sing with me, all of us singing together.
They love my voice: I can feel it, I know it.
I stretch for a harmony, hope I can make it,
and do, racing over the notes like a white-water raft
in a flooded river. And then down low:
no one knew I could sing this low.
My voice is the fullness of underwater,
the secret wendings of schools of fish,
the path of the whale after the fluke slaps
and she dives to depths rich as molasses.
Then up we soar like sailboats, up like gulls,
up the stairs and up and up, like bubbles in a glass
we rise, like tadpoles learning to breathe the air.

In the dim, stumbling hours of morning
a trapezoid of light outwits the kitchen blinds,
flares amber in my tea, and I remember:
something about a stairway with a landing,
something about myself as a beautiful singer,
and the music that wells up, naturally as breath,
even as we crush our lives, not listening.

THE HISTORY OF WOMEN

It was Annie Oakley you wanted, mother.
You said I bore a resemblance.
She rode on my Wild West training cup,
Her round, red sleeves billowing in the wind
As she aimed and fired, astride an indifferent pony.
You called me your own little cowgirl,
As if I could drink in trace levels of her essence,
And grow up a perfect shot.

She never missed. I did.
I called home from a Greyhound station in Oklahoma,
Wounded and pregnant,
Watched my last quarter slide into that cold metal slot
And waited for your answer.
Instead I heard a river of voices,
The static of a thousand conversations,
Like angels repeating the names of the dead.

"This is the story of all of us," I thought,
Picturing Annie Oakley's urgent telegram:
No one boarding the last steam engine West
To her rescue, hatbox in hand,
No one giving her a leg up
Into the red velvet coach,
No one putting a ticket in her gloved palm,
No cucumber sandwiches
In her small room above the saloon.

You said she was part of my blood;
I'd find her deep in my heart;
But that waiting room's full
Of warbrides and mail-order brides,
Runaway teenagers, coalminer's wives,
Seamstresses, suffragettes, secret smokers,
Riveters, writers and waitresses.
They spin like the eggs of a butchered chicken
A spiral around the ovaries,
Tiny and perfectly formed.

Now when you tell my daughter the stories,
It always sounds worse than it was:
Someone voted, someone died, and so on.
A baby is born. A star falls from the sky.

THE SATISFACTION OF A WOMAN COMBING

... It must
Be the finding of a satisfaction, and may
Be of a man skating, a woman dancing, a woman
Combing. The poem of the act of the mind.
                    —Wallace Stevens, *"Of Modern Poetry"*

Such a swift action, I barely think of it,
Imprinted in my catalogue of movements,
Automatic as pouring water in a glass,
Catching a baseball, easing out the clutch,
Lifting a baby, typing. When I was five
I stood in line, unwavering from my place,
On the wooden stage of the empty auditorium
Behind Talitha's plastic-clipped braids.
Mrs. Parker stooped to dispense,
In a movement as careful as the placing of eggs
Or scissors into the hands of children,
Black combs, from a black-painted coffee can.
I almost thought I wouldn't get one, but
Sure as the hurricane that took out our town
She delivered it, pressed the Unbreakable
Into my palm, and I did not drop it.
The tip of one tooth was clear, from a swirl
Of clear plastic somehow mixed in. Lucky.
Strummed, it sang of bamboo; it bent
But so far in an arch of teeth, then snapped back.
In angular strokes that abraded my ears,
I pulled it through cornsilk, again and again,
Approaching the painted backdrop of books,
And the flash of the silver umbrella,
To make a lasting impression.

Now it is action immersed in memory,
Noticed only when snagging,
Just as I only notice the hammer's slow swing
When the nail bends. What imperceptible
Mental revision goes on then?
Always, I stop for an instant,
Let that trajectory correct itself,
To be ready next time, at perfect pitch,
Just as my lips contract, my fingers arch,
For the right low note on the flute:
Satisfaction, a thousand corrections,
Weaving an action to absolute.

BODILY REPAIRS

I'm all the way back in the tilting chair,
The taste of nickels in my mouth,
And a stranger's clamps and fingers: Mr. Fix-it
Is patching disasters again, poking at potholes,
Tamping tar in the cracks of this bowling ball
Where I keep my good sense, my home.
It never looks better when he's done.
On my forehead he plasters the warning:
More work will be needed soon.
I'll chuck the bills in a drawer full of things:
Old glasses with lenses thinner than I can wear,
Old photographs of lovers, old wedding rings.

The broken limb heals with a little twist,
A slight limp, an ache for rainy days,
A scar where the rupture closed itself—
Knitting overtime to patch the leak—
But still, the patch is there, unsightly, numb.
Unlined, it cuts a gash across your palm.
Unhaired, it weaves its way across your leg.
Pink as a newborn, untanned pockmark,
Careless zigzag seam.
Softer than skin, it ripples against the grain.

Snakes shed their skins; perhaps that's wise,
Scrapping the entire enterprise,
Writing off the old life for the new.
The message shucks its envelope,
A papery missive, secondhand suicide note,
And crawls away clean, its whole body one scar.
Even the lens of the eye sheds, left behind,
Scraped loose on the bark of a tree or deep in a well.
It must be odd to feel your skin coming off.
It's nothing you can stop.
                              But after the battle,
You're one year older, with one more story to rattle.

A GRAY DAY IN FEBRUARY TO DISCUSS PLATH'S SUICIDE

February 11, 1994, Columbus, Ohio

My car is encased in a chrysalis of ice.
Icicles weld it to the ice-welded pavement,
Tied like the woman who must pay the rent
Left to flail on blue-black railroad tracks.
The windshield's cobbled glass, a doctor's door.
Ice in lava globs, streamers, signatures;
Ocean water dragging the sand
Gray, slick and clear, a cold cement floor.
Packed ice chocks the wheels behind the mudguard,
And my tires are already bald.
It's 22 below in the Erie salt mines,
The railroad couplings won't shunt:
Columbus has run out of salt,
Pipes have frozen and marriages failed.
Chip, kick, heat the key with a lighter.
Unusual news at six: prodigal weather:
Dogs, cars, whole houses
Splintered and carried away by the river,
Or snow as deep as cattle's ears.
A woman is found, bound and gagged in the deep freeze,
Her eyelashes frosted together.
Cars slide around on the highway
Like dancers, spinning slowly.
There isn't a name for what falls from the sky now.
It catches up to you like a dark horse—
The new heart arrives in a cooler of diamonds.
At last, it cracks. There, it's broken;
The numb thumb's burned.

FREESIAS: AN OPENING

for Elizabeth King

On my way to the gallery, I'm stopped
by rows of white freesia bouquets at a sidewalk stand.
Imported from a growing field in Africa,
They hold October air, cellophane wrapped,
Braced against black Manhattan, petal membrane
Thinner, finer than eggshell porcelain.
Spidery stems spin fractal progressions
From overblown funnel to tiniest unopen bud.

Elizabeth's figurines wait in glass boxes at Allan Stone,
Bisqued faces serene, doll-perfect above
The naked clockwork of their skeletons.
It took seven years, she said, to cast the right green
    bones.
Copper ribs sketch the framework
that glided beneath the skin of a loved one.
The extremities are porcelain, without collar,
Cuffs, or hem, to protect the line
Where prosthetics end and the bones begin.
They're technical remains: bolted, clamped
To lab stands for reviewing.
"M" is Elizabeth's mother, spirit distilled,
Same skull-curve, ice-blue eyes, tiny gloves;
On cheeks and lips, the faintest bloom of rose.
Another bust, the artist. At my footstep,
The head quivers slightly on its wooden stem.

At the party later, she laughs:
"Another seven years before a show."
But these things will grace the world
Long after we are gone.
Wrapped in the black coat for windy days,
She looks ready for the studio.
Elizabeth, these flowers are for you.

VALENTINE

What can we pack in this chocolate box
To spare your heart more fracture? There must be
Talismans to temper love's adventures.

A compass, with a fine bone
Needle on the lodestone. Phalanges
Of Saint Francis, for instance.

A flashlight, distance indomitable.
In its arc, men's hearts are translucent
As glycerin soap, mercilessly readable.

A patch-kit is useless in these situations.
Better to have armor of leather, lined
With hummingbird feathers.

Saint Joan sends you her silver spurs,
Says she admires your fire;
Wishes you better luck than hers.

Here's sycamore sap for the spirit level,
Wire cutters for traps,
Darwin's dice, and the little red dress.

Sadly, love must have electric storms
To operate properly. Sweetheart,
Listen to mother: wear your rubbers.

BAT

She woke in the night to that blue
Light slatting through bamboo shades;
A foreign room, a man whose name was new,
The light in stripes across his face, his hair
Long, blond, unwound from its string,
His breathing slow and even.
Pulled from the depths by barking dogs,
Or raccoons in trashcans, or the sound
Of the wind in linden trees,
She rose to touch the things on his dresser:
The smooth wallet, bent to his curve,
The pearl pocket knife, the dried maple leaf,
Tickets, his soft scarf, a bicycle bell,
And a bat trapped in a lucite cube.
From its block of ice, it stared at her.
Cramped in perpetual half-flight,
Wings close to its body, fangs bared,
Velvet fur beaded with air:
A handful of life that would bite.
Did he find it, crumpled in the rain gutter,
wrapped like a cigar among fallen leaves,
And stop to unfurl the damp parcel with his fingers,
Pulling the dead wings out, the small mouth open,
Carrying the treasure home in his palm
To casket in a simile of flight?
Or was it frozen that way as it died,
Trapped in a box, flapping
Like a flame-burnt moth, until
The plastic resin sealed its lungs?
Perhaps he had nothing to do with it—
A hundred bats a day are smothered
In a souvenir plant in Mexico
Where the small ones who fall sideways,
Or sink as if sleeping, are pitched on a heap,
Useless in their imperfect endings.
Atop each wing, three filigree fingers
Curled like the hand of a fetus.

She wanted to ask him if he had done this,
But he lay still, arms wrapped in the sheet,
Knees bent, as if flying through his sleep,
Swirled in shadows cast like tea leaves:
A future she couldn't read.

PROGRESS COMES, BUT NOT TO BRUNSWICK COUNTY, VIRGINIA

for Richard Hammack

Last winter we walked the woods on his parents' farm,
Followed Shining Creek to the old stone dam
Which slaves had built and frost had heaved and broken,
The half-hewn grindstone boulder rugged with moss,
The chink holes in the millrace home for birds.
We sat by the creek in a bank of ferns and laughed.
"Buckminster Fuller's geodesic map
  Fits the world's space to triangles,
  More accurate than orange peels," he said,
"Although, it's obsolete; no bookstores sell it."
  I pictured his apartment in Chapel Hill:
  The closet would hold rows of blue jeans, white shirts—
  No quandaries for Richard; he always picks vanilla.
  Beneath the paintings glazed in green and blue
  His new computer tumbles an image sketched
  In light: Richard is now a man of math.
"Four dimensional structures can be designed,
  In analogs of three dimensional forms.
  The shape's a homotopy, shifting, blending,
  Sometimes collapsing into one thin edge."
"Can you build it?" I asked, watching his hands
  Describe lines in air like circling a globe.
"Oh, no," he said, and smiled. "But it exists—
  In that mathematical reality."
  Cliff swallows dipped for milkweed for their nests,
  Daubing the weeds with mud from the bank of the creek.
"If we get anything we want," I said, half joking,
"You realize, we can never live here again."
  In our hometown, nothing ever changes,
  Except the creek has moved away from the dam,
  And from his parents' porch we can see, at night,
  The lights of the encroaching shopping mall.
"I know," he said. "I know." And we went home.

FELLOW TRAVELER

I see you, fetus, feta ball floating in brine;
A bun in the oven, half-baked, still dough in the middle,
Hairless humanoid, safe in your space capsule,
Observing the glow, listening to my heart.
That it is enough for you flatters me.
You dance to the music I make in my sleep,
Audience within the sounding board.
All other voices boom bass, like noisy neighbors
Having a party they haven't invited you to, yet.
You are the next guest to enter the room.
Come, swim in our medium, drink our air!
Come meet the one who's held you for so long.

NEW SNOW

We start up Fifth, leave tracks beside
The Olentangy, trailing through
Campus and beyond. The river
Is dark, black, shot with gold
From the lights; the moon is lost in a cloud.
The asphalt is dormant under our feet,
Our steps absorbed in white.

Trees seep into the clouds,
Their ink deeper than sky or river.
We swing west, where I ran in summer,
Between the high green rows of corn,
Now stubble, frozen under a sheet
As thick and white as pool room smoke,
Snow lighting our faces like day.

We race across the furrows, reach
The edge of the woods, and stumble in.
Quiet rings through the stand of trees.
He heats up a cigarette, smoke
Burning from its orange mouth
Like so much breath. My breath
Is smoke, too, tonight.

"The last time," he says, going on
With the story, a long one, about
The last time. "Been there," I say.
He hunches his shoulders up to his cold ears,
And I just enjoy the sound of his voice,
The brush of leather as he swings his arms.
"It's a beautiful thing," he says.

We're at the highway now, but no one
Dares that gray slush at this hour.
A good steady rhythm works up as we walk;
We could go on walking forever.
He lives here, always lived here, always
Knows the way when we drive somewhere.
I've never had to tell him yet.

RESTLESS

I

People move slowly, as if through liquid.
They are slow to take each other in their arms.
They are slow to speak of love. They speak too late.
We see only the glass half-empty in the empty room,
The heavy velvet curtain holding back the light.
A man walks in. The phone rings:
The same sound in every house in this city.
He picks it up. No answer.
Ice tinkles in his glass. There are implications.
He utters the name of the woman he loves,
And no one hears it.

II

He's gone. She swallows the lime rind whole,
Licks salt from the edge of his glass,
And curls up on the love seat, like a garden slug,
To dry out. The man with the whiskey sour eyes,
The man with the Ouzo tongue,
Still spar at each other, but have forgotten her.
Narrow as a promise in her blue sequined sheath,
She's radiant as ever, a lightbulb
With a filament trembling inside.
And oh, her smile's an electrical field—
Fluorescent lights glow around her!
But she must never drink again.
She stills her fingertips with a thought:
The young man, sequestered in the barn
Like the meat of a walnut,
Once rested his head on her shoulder.

III

He paces the floor of the tackroom,
From bed to typewriter, punching bag
To mother's steamer trunk.
Dark hair wild, the color of coal,
Porcelain face chiseled just shy of caricature.
He is practicing grief with the will of a Samurai.
Stripped of his shirt, he's muscled smooth,
A cork in the water, fatherless boy, orphan man.
Below him, the horses move in their stalls,
Rumbling when they dream of his hands.
Cursed in love with his own half-sister,
He sighs, and the world sighs back.

LAMENT FOR PANGAEA

In the night, Brazil mourns Cameroon.
Longing for the soft fit, before the drift,
Harmonic wholeness, one edge, one wavesong,
Gulfless, the heart's Pangaea.
Wegener, searching the mountains for shells,
Tries to explain:

Gondwana is gone, Laurasia.
Not sunk, no;
Just drifting away, cracking up.
You can call to each other, send waves,
Watch the stars, spawn tiny airplanes,
But never touch again.

In time, you will know a new shape. You will
Swim in oceans warmer than Panthalassa,
Spread to the ends of the earth, and rise
In mountain ranges where once was sea.
You will move on, the strata of another life
Recorded in your coast, a scar to remember it by.

NOTES

The following passage from "After Reading Neruda"

Oh corazón perdido
en mí mismo, en mi propia investidura,
qué generosa transición te puebla!

is from Pablo Neruda's poem "El Egoísta," found in *Jardin de Invierno*. I translate it as

Oh heart lost
inside my essence, inside my proper investiture,
what generous change inhabits you!

Los bancos del río means "the banks of the river." *El corazón* means "the heart." The noun is masculine in Spanish, but I have made the heart feminine in English, here.

Paseo is defined by American flamenco guitarist Paul Hecht, in his memoir *The Wind Cried* (1968), as "classical evening promenade of sweethearts or potential sweethearts in gardens, squares, or main streets."

"A Gray Day in February to Discuss Plath's Suicide" was inspired in part by Janet Malcolm's *The Silent Woman: Sylvia Plath and Ted Hughes* (1993), in which she recounts A. Alvarez's memoir of Plath, *The Savage God*, describing the harsh weather in England at the time of Plath's death:

The snow began just after Christmas and would not let up. By New Year the whole country had ground to a halt. The trains froze on the tracks, the abandoned trucks froze on the roads. . . . Water pipes froze solid; for a bath you had to scheme and cajole those rare friends with centrally heated houses. . . . The gas failed and Sunday roasts were raw. The lights failed and candles, of course, were unobtainable. Nerves failed and marriages crumbled. Finally, the heart failed.

Information about Pangaea is from Mary McNeil, ed., *The Earth Sciences Reference* (1991).